A BITTER TRIAL

A Bitter Trial

Evelyn Waugh
and
John Carmel Cardinal Heenan
on the
Liturgical Changes

Expanded Edition

Edited by
Alcuin Reid

IGNATIUS PRESS   SAN FRANCISCO

First published in 1996 by Saint Austin Press, England
© 1996 & 2000 by Alcuin Reid

Cover photograph by S. Smith Photogaphy, Chicago
("An anticipatory Mass in the older form of the Roman rite
for the Feast of the Exultation of Holy Cross at
Iglesia de San Ginés de Arlés
in Madrid on September 13, 2010.")

Cover design by Riz Boncan Marsella

ISBN 978-1-58617-522-1
Library of Congress Control Number 2011905245
Printed in the United States of America ∞

Dedicated
to the memory of

Francis Aloysius Doolan
1924–1986

Priest, mentor, and friend

Maybe he had doubts about the orders,
but [he] never had a doubt about obeying them.

Archbishop T. F. Little

Contents

Foreword

Joseph Pearce

"Much water has flown under Tiber's bridges," wrote Alec Guinness in his autobiography, "carrying away splendor and mystery from Rome, since the Pontificate of Pius XII." Writing in the mid-eighties, Guinness lamented the "banality and vulgarity of the translations which have ousted the sonorous Latin and little Greek" from the liturgy and regretted that "[h]andshaking and embarrassed smiles or smirks have replaced the older courtesies." Although dismayed by the nature of the liturgical changes, Guinness was sure that the Church would recover from such nonsense, "so long as the God who is worshipped is the God of all ages, past and to come, and not the Idol of Modernity, so venerated by some of our bishops, priests and miniskirted nuns".[1]

Even as Guinness was lamenting the chaos that followed in the wake of the Second Vatican Council, there were signs that the Church was recovering from the modernist encroachments that had sought to marry her to what Waugh, in his article in the *Spectator* that opens

[1] Alec Guinness, *Blessings in Disguise* (London: Hamish Hamilton, 1985), p. 45.

the present volume, had rightly called "our own deplorable epoch".[2]

A spirit of restoration had been heralded in 1978 by the election of John Paul II to the papacy. Schooled in modern philosophy, yet a man of deep love for the ancient faith, Pope John Paul II attempted to implement a more faithful interpretation of the Second Vatican Council, which called for a renewal, rather than a deconstruction, of the liturgy. Thereafter the beauty and authority of Tradition, presumed dead after Vatican II, began to show signs of resurrection.

Perhaps, with the wisdom of hindsight, we can now see the election of John Paul II as the date at which the high tide of the modernist encroachment within the Church began to turn. Yet there was always the danger that John Paul's successor would lack the courage or the ability to continue with the "reform of the reform". Would the next pope exercise his power to exorcise the darkness? With this question looming ominously over the Church, it is no wonder that faithful Catholics around the world leapt for joy when they heard the news that Joseph Cardinal Ratzinger had been elected pope. Their exhilaration, and their exhalation of a deep sigh of relief, at Pope Benedict's accession to the Throne of Peter helped to soften the sorrow at the passing of his illustrious predecessor. Mixed with the grief was the joyful

---

[2] "The Same Again, Please"; see p. 35. All page numbers given in the footnotes refer to the present volume if no publication information is given.

confidence that the Church and her sacred liturgy were in safe hands.

Yet, in the light of this resurrection of liturgical Tradition within the Church, it is important that we remember the darkness from which the Church is now emerging, and the suffering it caused to many faithful Catholics who found themselves seemingly deserted in the gloom. As Alcuin Reid reminds us in his introduction to this volume, "the 'bitter trial' that tested the faith of Evelyn Waugh and so many of his generation, as well as the almost-impossible situation in which Cardinal Heenan and many other clergy found themselves, must not be forgotten." [3] And, lest we forget, let's remind ourselves of the background to Waugh's conversion to Catholicism and the reason that he remained faithful to the Church and her Tradition.

On 21 August 1930 Waugh had written to the Jesuit Martin D'Arcy that he had come to the realization that the Catholic Church was "the only genuine form of Christianity [and] that Christianity is the essential and formative constituent of western culture". [4] Six weeks later, on 29 September, Father D'Arcy received Waugh into the Church. In the wake of his conversion and the controversy it caused, Waugh wrote an article for the *Daily Express* explaining his reasons for becoming a Catholic:

[3] See p. 25.
[4] Quoted in Selina Hastings, *Evelyn Waugh: A Biography* (London: Minerva, 1994), p. 225.

It seems to me that in the present phase of European history the essential issue is no longer between Catholicism, on one side, and Protestantism, on the other, but between Christianity and Chaos. . . .

Today we can see it on all sides as the active negation of all that western culture has stood for. Civilization—and by this I do not mean talking cinemas and tinned food, nor even surgery and hygienic houses, but the whole moral and artistic organization of Europe—has not in itself the power of survival. It came into being through Christianity, and without it has no significance or power to command allegiance. The loss of faith in Christianity and the consequential lack of confidence in moral and social standards have become embodied in the ideal of a materialistic, mechanized state. . . . It is no longer possible . . . to accept the benefits of civilization and at the same time deny the supernatural basis upon which it rests.

Asserting that "Christianity is essential to civilization and that it is in greater need of combative strength than it has been for centuries", Waugh argued that "Christianity exists in its most complete and final form in the Roman Catholic Church." [5] On 8 October 1930 the *Bystander* observed of Waugh's conversion that "the brilliant young author [was] the latest man of letters to be received into the Catholic Church. Other well-known literary people who have gone over to Rome include Sheila Kaye-Smith, Compton MacKenzie, Alfred Noyes, Father Ronald Knox and G. K. Chesterton." The

[5] Evelyn Waugh, "Converted to Rome: Why It Has Happened to Me", *Daily Express*, 20 October 1930.

list was far from exhaustive. By the 1930s the rising tide of converts to Catholicism had become a torrent. Throughout that decade there were some twelve thousand converts a year in England alone.

The burgeoning Catholic revival was also flourishing in the United States. A few weeks after Waugh's reception into the Church, G. K. Chesterton was in New York debating with the famous Chicago lawyer Clarence Darrow. The debate was entitled "Will the World Return to Religion?" An audience of four thousand heard both sides of the debate and then voted on the question. The result was 2,359 for Chesterton's point of view and 1,022 for Darrow's. Meanwhile, in Europe, there was a wave of literary converts to rival that in England. These included François Mauriac, Léon Bloy, Jacques Maritain, Charles Péguy, Henri Ghéon, Giovanni Papini, Gertrud von le Fort, and Sigrid Undset, all of whom were either converts or else reverts who had lost their faith but had returned to the Church.

It is a singularly intriguing fact that the preconciliar Church was so effective in evangelizing modern culture, whereas the number of converts to the faith seemed to diminish in the sixties and seventies in direct proportion to the presence of the much-vaunted *aggiornamento*, the muddle-headed belief that the Church needed to be brought "up-to-date". The success of orthodoxy in winning converts compared with the failure of modernism must surely raise not merely eyebrows but soul-searching questions. The facts would appear to confirm the maxim usually attributed to Chesterton that we don't need a Church that will move with the world but a Church that will move the world. This discrepancy between ancient faith and modern innovation was the backdrop to Waugh's increasingly enraged engagement with the winds of modernism that seemed to be taking the Church by storm in the sixties, a storm that shed its ominous and gloomy darkness over the final years of his life. This volume, so meticulously and conscientiously edited by Alcuin Reid, documents Waugh's suffering and shows the enormity of the damage done to the timeless liturgy of the Church by the vernacularizing vandals and *aggiornamento* agitators of the sixties.

Waugh collapsed and died on Easter Sunday 1966, only an hour or so after attending a private Latin Mass celebrated by his friend Philip Caraman, S.J. His daughter wrote to Lady Diana Cooper of the "wonderful miracle" of grace that attended her father in his final hours: "Don't be too upset about Papa. I think it was a kind of wonderful miracle. You know how he longed to die and dying as he did on Easter Sunday, when all the liturgy is about death and resurrection, after a Latin Mass and holy communion would be exactly as he wanted. I am sure he had prayed for death at Mass. I am very, very happy for him." [6]

In his panegyric at the requiem Mass at Westminster Cathedral, Father Caraman emphasized the place of the Mass at the very heart of Waugh's life and faith:

> The Mass mattered for him most in his world. During the greater part of his lifetime it remained as it

[6] See p. 98.

had done for centuries, the same and everywhere recognizable, when all else was threatened with change. He was sad when he read of churches in which the old altar was taken down and a table substituted, or of side altars abolished as private Masses were held to be unliturgical or unnecessary. With all who know something of the pattern of history, he was perturbed.[7]

Waugh's love for the Mass is evident throughout this volume, and the "bitter trial" documented in the following pages serves as a witness of the real suffering that Waugh and other Tradition-oriented Catholics experienced during those dismally dark days. As the timeless and priceless inheritance of the Church was being squandered by clueless modernists, the faithful clung to the Church with dogged and dogmatic determination. Now, after this dark night of the Church's collective soul, we are beginning to see the restoration of the liturgy for which Waugh hoped and prayed.

[7] See p. 101.

Introduction

The first edition of this small book appeared in the pontificate of Pope John Paul II, in the wake of the 1996 "Oxford Declaration on Liturgy", which asserted that "the preconciliar liturgical movement as well as the manifest intentions of *Sacrosanctum Concilium* have in large part been frustrated by powerful contrary forces, which could be described as bureaucratic, philistine and secularist. The effect has been to deprive the Catholic people of much of their liturgical heritage." [1]

This was somewhat of a bold assertion. It was, however, based on a reality that, if not widely acknowledged at the time, was certainly known: not all went well with the postconciliar liturgical reform.

The discovery that occasioned this book—four previously unpublished letters from the English writer Evelyn Waugh (1903–1966) to John Cardinal Heenan (1905–1975), archbishop of Liverpool from 1957 until his promotion to Westminster in 1963, in the papers of the latter—was a small-enough find. Yet they, and the other letters and documents herein assembled around them (to which in this third edition another seven are added), paint a vivid picture of two men, faithful and

---

[1] Quoted in Stratford Caldecott, ed., *Beyond the Prosaic: Renewing the Liturgical Movement* (T&T Clark, 1998), p. 163.

obedient to the Church, whose better judgement—
and for at least one of them, his very faith—was severely
put to the test by the liturgical changes imposed in
the wake of the Second Vatican Council, and even
those that came before.[2]

Evelyn Waugh was no reactionary fool. His concern about rowdiness in church[3] shows that he readily
recognised the all-too-common misinterpretation of the
Second Vatican Council's call for *participatio actuosa*
(actual participation):[4] an emphasis on external action
without sufficient regard for that unobservable, essentially contemplative, participation of the mind and heart
that must have priority.

Similarly, he was well aware that the Latin tongue,
or any sacred language for that matter, is no barrier to
actual participation in the liturgy. He rightly reacted
against the wave of vernacularisation breaking over the
liturgy to an extent nowhere called for by the Council. And he appreciated that to change ritual is to risk
altering the faith, particularly that of simple folk.

[2] In a letter dated 9 December 1963, Heenan wrote: "If I were given
a personal preference, I would not want any change in the ceremonies as
I much preferred the old Holy Week ceremonies to those we have at
present" (Archive of the Archbishop of Westminster [AAW], HE). The
liturgical reforms enacted between 1948 and 1962—of which the 1955
Holy Week reform, which Waugh found so repugnant, is the best known—
require further study and evaluation today.

[3] See, for example, Waugh's letter to Lady Daphne Acton, 15 March
1963, p. 44.

[4] Second Vatican Council, Constitution on the Sacred Liturgy, *Sacrosanctum Concilium*, no. 14. The phrase is translated here as "actual participation", less misleadingly than the usual English rendering of "active
participation". Cf. further: Joseph Ratzinger, *The Feast of Faith: Approaches
to a Theology of the Liturgy* (Ignatius Press, 1986), pp. 68ff.

At the time of the Council, clergy and laity were proud of their loyalty and obedience to ecclesiastical authority. Being faithful to Christ and to His Church meant, above all, doing what one was told by authority. Although they may at times have "had doubts about the orders", they "never had a doubt about obeying them".[5] Certainly this was true for Cardinal Heenan; as he wrote in 1969: "If the Holy Father has decided to reform the liturgy, we must accept."[6]

Indeed, there was an uncritical assumption abroad that the liturgical changes were not only authoritatively to be obeyed but were divinely inspired (the corollary being that to resist them was to oppose God's will). As Heenan wrote to one correspondent: "If the Pope and the bishops of the whole world have agreed on these changes the Holy Spirit must be guiding His Church";[7] and to another: "When the voice of the whole Church speaks, we have to stifle our personal preferences and accept the fact that the Holy Ghost is guiding the Church." This letter concludes: "Reserve judgement for a few years and you will see why God has led the Church to a new liturgy."[8]

Heenan's correspondence reveals the tightrope walked by this pastor as he sought to be faithful to the measures Rome required him to implement, as well as to

---

[5] Archbishop T. F. Little, homily at the funeral Mass for Father Francis Aloysius Doolan, Saint Mary's Church, East Malvern, Victoria, Australia, 16 April 1986.

[6] Letter dated 8 March 1969, AAW, HE.

[7] Letter dated 1 December 1965, AAW, HE.

[8] Letter dated 18 December 1963, AAW, HE.

the sentiments and needs of his people—and indeed to his own. His papers indicate that he struggled to balance differing views on the liturgy for years. They contain an abundance of replies to people worried about the changes. An early example:

> Nobody could be more attached to the Latin Mass than myself. But when the Holy See gives directions we have to obey them. You must not think that the vernacular is a whim of the bishops or that the English hierarchy has been left much option in this matter.[9]

A later one:

> You have my sympathy. I know exactly how you feel. It is a pity that the Mass had to be altered but it seems that all the liturgists are agreed that the ceremonies must be simplified and made more like the primitive Mass.[10]

Later still Cardinal Heenan obtained a singular concession from Pope Paul VI for the continued celebration of an older form of the Mass for those who wanted it. Whilst he was an obedient agent of change, Heenan could not abandon those who, like himself, felt the burden of those changes deeply.

The permissions received to use previously published and archival material are gratefully acknowledged, including those granted by the Archive of the Archbishop of Westminster, the Department of Manuscripts of the British Library, Miss Claudia Fitzherbert, the Peters Fraser & Dunlop Group Ltd., Mr. and

---

[9] Letter dated 17 December 1964, AAW, HE.
[10] Letter dated 29 April 1967, AAW, HE.

Mrs. Auberon Waugh, and Weidenfeld & Nicholson. Also gratefully acknowledged is the assistance of Daniel Coughlan and Dom Alban Nunn, O.S.B., in the compilation of this third edition; the archival research used here, though, is entirely my own. I am profoundly grateful to Joseph Pearce for his kind foreword, and to the Countess of Oxford for her gracious afterword.

As the "revival of the liturgical movement and the initiation of a new cycle of reflection and reform" [11] continues—now with added impetus in the light of the pontificate of Pope Benedict XVI—the "bitter trial" that tested the faith of Evelyn Waugh and so many of his generation, as well as the almost-impossible situation in which Cardinal Heenan and many other clergy found themselves, must not be forgotten. Whilst Waugh was, sadly, all too correct when he wrote in his last letter on the subject, "I shall not live to see it [the beauty of the liturgy] restored", we owe it to the sacrifices made by his generation, as we owe it to our own and indeed to those to come, to see to it that their sufferings, and their insights presented herein, were not in vain.

Alcuin Reid

15th August 2011

---

[11] "The Oxford Declaration on Liturgy", quoted in Caldecott, *Beyond the Prosaic*, p. 164.

Evelyn Waugh—
"The Same Again, Please"*

It is unlikely that the world's politicians are following the concluding sessions of the Vatican Council with the anxious scrutiny given to its opening stages in 1869. Then the balance of power in Europe was precariously dependent on the status of the Papal States in Italy; France and Austria directly, Prussia indirectly, and the Piedmontese kingdom particularly, were involved in their future. Even Protestant England was intent. Gladstone had his own, personal, theological preoccupations and was in unofficial correspondence with Lord Acton, but Lord Clarendon, the Foreign Minister, and most of the Cabinet studied the dispatches of their agent, Odo Russell (lately selected and edited with the title of *The Roman Question*), and pressed him for the fullest details. Manning was privately dispensed from his vow of secrecy in order that he might keep Russell informed. Queen Victoria ruled as many Catholics as Anglicans, a section of whom in Ireland were proving increasingly troublesome.

The Council, as is well known, adjourned in dramatic circumstances which seemed to presage disaster. Subsequent history confirmed its decisions. The Paris

* *Spectator* [*The Spectator*], 23 November 1962, pp. 785–88.

Commune obliterated Gallicanism. Bismark's *Kultur-kampf* alienated all respectable support of the dissident Teutons. All that Odo Russell had consistently predicted came about in spite of the wishes of the European statesmen.

The consultations, resumed after their long recess and dignified by the title of the Second Vatican Council, are not expected to have the same direct influence outside the Church. The popular newspapers have caught at phrases in the Pope's utterances to suggest that there is a prospect of the reunion of Christendom. Most Christians, relying on the direct prophecies of Our Lord, expect this to occur in some moment of historical time. Few believe that moment to be imminent. The Catholic aspiration is that the more manifest the true character of the Church can be made, the more the dissenters will be drawn to make their submission. There is no possibility of the Church modifying her defined doctrines to attract those to whom they are repugnant. The Orthodox Churches of the East, with whom the doctrinal differences are small and technical, are more hostile to Rome than are the Protestants. To them the sack and occupation of Constantinople for the first half of the thirteenth century—an event which does not bulk large in the historical conspectus of the West—is as lively and bitter a memory as is Hitler's persecution of the Jews. Miracles are possible; it is presumptuous to expect them; only a miracle can reconcile the East with Rome.

With the Reformed Churches, among whom the Church of England holds a unique position, in that most of its members believe themselves to be a part of the

Catholic Church of the West, social relations are warmer but intellectual differences are exacerbated. A century ago Catholics were still regarded as potential traitors, as ignorant, superstitious and dishonest, but there was a common ground in the acceptance of the authority of Scripture and the moral law. Nowadays, I see it stated, representative Anglican clergymen withhold their assent to such rudimentary Christian tenets as the virgin birth and resurrection of Our Lord; in the recent prosecution of *Lady Chatterley's Lover* two eminent Anglican divines gave evidence for the defence, one of them, a bishop, in the most imprudent terms. Another Anglican dignitary has given his approval to the regime which is trying to extirpate Christianity in China. Others have given their opinion that a man who believes himself threatened by a painful death may commit suicide. Aberrations such as these, rather than differences in the interpretation of the Augustinian theory of Grace, are grave stumbling blocks to understanding.

It is possible that the Council will announce a definition of the *communicatio in sacris* with members of other religious societies which is forbidden to Catholics. Rigour is the practice of some dioceses, laxity of others. There is no universal rule, for example, about the celebration of mixed marriages. On the other hand, some French priests, in an excess of 'togetherness', are said to administer Communion to non-Catholics, an imprudence, if not a sacrilege, which can only be reprobated. The personal cordiality shown by the Pope to Protestants may well be the prelude to official encouragement to co-operate in social and humanitarian

activities, which would remove bitterness from a con-
demnation of association in the sacraments.

The question of Anglican Orders is unlikely to be
raised, but it is worth noting that the conditions have
changed since their validity was condemned. Then the
matter was judged on the historical evidence of the
Reformation settlement. But since then there have been
goings-on with *episcopi-vagantes*, Jansenist Dutch and
heterodox eastern bishops, with the result that an incal-
culable proportion of Anglican clergy may in fact be
priests. They may themselves produce individual apostolic, genealogical trees, but the results will be of little
interest to the more numerous Protestant bodies to
whom the Pope's paternal benevolence is equally
directed.

A Catholic believes that whatever is enacted at the
Council will ultimately affect the entire human race,
but its immediate purposes are domestic—the setting
in order of the household rudely disturbed in 1870.
There are many questions of great importance to the
constitution of the Church which do not directly affect
the ordinary Catholic layman—the demarcation of dioceses, the jurisdiction of bishops, the setting to contemporary uses of the powers of the ancient religious
orders, the changes necessary in seminaries to render
them more attractive and more effective, the adapta-
tion of missionary countries to their new national
status, and so forth. These can safely be left to the
experience and statesmanship of the Fathers of the
Council. But in the preliminary welcome which
the project has enjoyed during the past three years

there has been an insistent note that the "Voice of the Laity" shall be more clearly heard and that voice, so far as it has been audible in northern Europe and the United States, has been largely of the minority who demand radical reform. It seems to me possible that many of the assembled Fathers, whatever their own predictions, have an uneasy feeling that there is a powerful body of the laity urging them to decisions which are, in fact, far from the hopes of the larger but less vocal body of the faithful.

I speak for no one but myself, but I believe I am fairly typical of English Catholics. The fact that I was brought up in another society does not embarrass me. I have been a Catholic for thirty-two of what are technically known as my "years of reason"; longer, I think, than many of the 'progressives'; moreover, I think that a large proportion of European Catholics, despite their baptisms and first communions, are in fact "converts" in the sense that there came to them at some stage of adolescence or maturity the moment of private decision between acceptance and rejection of the Church's claims.

I believe that I am typical of that middle rank of the Church, far from her leaders, much farther from her saints; distinct, too, from the doubting, defiant, despairing souls who perform so conspicuously in contemporary fiction and drama. We take little part, except where our personal sympathies are aroused, in the public life of the Church, in her countless pious and benevolent institutions. We hold the creeds, we attempt to observe the moral law, we go to Mass on days of obligation and glance rather often at the vernacular translations of the Latin, we contribute to the support of the clergy. We seldom have any direct contact with the hierarchy. We go to some inconvenience to educate our children in the faith. We hope to die fortified by the last rites. In every age we have formed the main body of "the faithful" and we believe that it was for us, as much as for the saints and for the notorious sinners, that the Church was founded. Is it our voice that the Conciliar Fathers are concerned to hear?

There are three questions of their authority which sometimes come to our attention.

One is the Index of Prohibited Books. I have been told that its promulgation depends upon the discretion of the diocesan bishop. I do not know if it has been promulgated in my diocese. It is not at all easy to obtain a copy. When found, it is very dull, consisting largely of pamphlets and theses on forgotten controversies. It does not include most of the anthropological, Marxist and psychological theses which, uncritically read, might endanger faith and morals. Nor, as is popularly believed, does it include absurdities like *Alice in Wonderland*. There are a few works, such as Addison's Essays, which one expects to find in any reputable home and several which are compulsory reading at the universities, but in general it is not a troublesome document. Sartre's presence on the list provides a convenient excuse for not reading him. But there is an obvious anomaly in preserving a legal act which is generally disregarded. I think most laymen would be glad if the Fathers of the Council would consider whether the Index has any relevance in the modern world; whether it would not be better to give a general warning of dangerous reading and to allow confessors to decide in individual cases, while retaining particular censorship only over technical books of theology which might be mistaken for orthodox teaching.

A second point is the procedure of ecclesiastical courts. Most laymen spend a lifetime without being involved with them, just as they live without acquaintance with criminal proceedings. Cases of nullity of marriage are, however, becoming more common and much vexation and often grave suffering is caused by the long delays which result from the congestion of the courts and from their laborious methods. The layman does not question the authority of the law or the justice of the decisions; it is simply that when he finds himself in doubt, he thinks he should know in a reasonable time his precise legal status.

Thirdly, it would be satisfactory to know the limits of the personal authority held by the bishop over the laity. No vows of obedience have been made. Not in England, but in many parts of the world it is common to see a proclamation enjoining the faithful "on pain of mortal sin" to vote in a parliamentary election or abstain from certain entertainments. Have our bishops in fact the right to bandy threats of eternal damnation in this way?

As the months pass and the Council becomes engrossed in its essential work, it is likely that the secular press will give less attention to it than it has done to its spectacular assembly. The questions for discussion are a matter of speculation to all outside the inner circle but there is a persistent rumour that changes may be made in the liturgy. I lately heard the sermon of an enthusiastic, newly ordained priest who spoke, perhaps with conscious allusion to Mr Macmillan's unhappy phrase about Africa, of a "great wind" that was to blow through us, sweeping away the irrelevant accretions of centuries and revealing the Mass in its pristine, apostolic simplicity; and as I considered his congregation, closely packed parishioners of a small country town, of whom I regard myself as a typical member, I thought how little his aspirations corresponded with ours.

Certainly none of us had ambitions to usurp his pulpit. There is talk in northern Europe and the United States of lay theologians. Certainly a number of studious men have read deeply in theology and are free with their opinions, but I know of none whose judgement I would prefer to that of the simplest parish priest. Sharp minds may explore the subtlest verbal problems, but in the long routine of the seminary and the life spent with the Offices of the Church the truth is most likely to emerge. It is worth observing that in the two periods when laymen took the most active part in theological controversy, those of Pascal and Acton, the laymen were wrong.

Still less do we aspire to usurp his place at the altar. "The Priesthood of the Laity" is a cant phrase of the decade and abhorrent to those of us who have met it. We claim no equality with our priests, whose personal failings and inferiorities (where they exist) serve only to emphasise the mystery of their unique calling. Anything in costume or manner or social habit that tends to disguise that mystery is something leading us away from the sources of devotion. The failure of the French "worker priests" is fresh in our memories. A man who grudges a special and higher position to another is very far from being a Christian.

As the service proceeded in its familiar way I wondered how many of us wanted to see any change. The church is rather dark. The priest stood rather far away. His voice was not clear and the language he spoke was not that of everyday use. This was the Mass for whose restoration the Elizabethan martyrs had gone to the scaffold. St Augustine, St Thomas à Becket, St Thomas More, Challoner and Newman would have been perfectly at their ease among us; were, in fact, present there with us. Perhaps few of us consciously considered this, but their presence and that of all the saints silently supported us. Their presence would not have been more palpable had we been making the responses aloud in the modern fashion.

It is not, I think, by a mere etymological confusion that the majority of English-speaking people believe that "venerable" means "old". There is a deep-lying connection in the human heart between worship and age. But the new fashion is for something bright and loud and practical. It has been set by a strange alliance between archaeologists absorbed in their speculations on the rites of the second century, and modernists who wish to give the Church the character of our own deplorable epoch. In combination they call themselves "liturgists".

The late Father Couturier, the French Dominican, was very active in enlisting the service of atheists in designing aids to devotion, but tourists are more common than worshippers in the churches he inspired. At Vence there is a famous little chapel designed in his extreme age by Matisse. It is always full of sightseers and the simple nursing sisters whom it serves are proud of the acquisition. But the Stations of the Cross, scrawled over a single wall, are so arranged that it is scarcely possible to make the traditional devotions before them. The sister in charge tries to keep the trippers from chattering but there is no one to disturb; on the occasions I have been there I have never seen anyone in prayer, as one always finds in dingy churches decorated with plaster and tinsel.

The new Catholic cathedral in Liverpool is circular in plan. The congregation are to be disposed in tiers, as though in a surgical operating theatre. If they raise their eyes they will be staring at one another. Backs are often distracting; faces will be more so. The intention is to bring everyone as near as possible to the altar. I wonder if the architect has studied the way in which people take their places at a normal parochial Mass. In all the churches with which I am familiar, it is the front pews which are filled last.

During the last few years we have experienced the triumph of the "liturgists" in the new arrangement of the services for the end of Holy Week and for Easter. For centuries these had been enriched by devotions which were dear to the laity—the anticipation of the morning office of Tenebrae, the vigil at the Altar of Repose, the Mass of the Presanctified. It was not how the Christians of the second century observed the season. It was the organic growth of the needs of the people. Not all Catholics were able to avail themselves of the services but hundreds did, going to live in or near the monastic houses and making an annual retreat which began with *Tenebrae* on Wednesday afternoon and ended about midday on Saturday with the anticipated Easter Mass. During those three days time was conveniently apportioned between the rites of the Church and the discourses of the priest taking the retreat, with little temptation to distraction. Now nothing happens before Thursday evening. All Friday morning is empty. There is an hour or so in church on Friday afternoon. All Saturday is quite blank until late at night. The Easter Mass is sung at midnight to a weary congregation who are constrained to "renew their baptismal vows" in the vernacular and later repair to bed. The significance of Easter as a feast of dawn is quite lost, as is the unique character of Christmas as the Holy Night. I have noticed in the monastery I frequent a marked falling-off in the number of retreatants since the innovations or, as the liturgists would prefer to call them, the restorations. It may well be that these services are nearer to the practice of primitive Christianity, but the Church rejoices in the development of dogma; why does it not also admit the development of liturgy? [1]

---

[1] Earlier in 1962 Waugh wrote to Lady Diana Cooper expressing his dissatisfaction with the post-1955 Holy Week rites. First, on March 30, in Lent: "The new liturgy leaves endless blank periods, particularly Holy Saturday"; and second, on Good Friday from Downside Abbey: "A very happy Easter to you in your new house or wherever you are. You are

There is a party among the hierarchy who wish to make superficial but startling changes in the Mass in order to make it more widely intelligible. The nature of the Mass is so profoundly mysterious that the most acute and holy men are continually discovering further nuances of significance. It is not a peculiarity of the Roman Church that much which happens at the altar is in varying degrees obscure to most of the worshippers. It is in fact the mark of all the historic, apostolic Churches. In some the liturgy is in a dead language such as Ge'ez or Syriac; in others in Byzantine Greek or Slavonic which differs greatly from the current speech of the people.

The question of the use of the vernacular has been debated until there is nothing new left to be said. In

---

constantly in my prayers here where, as usual, I am spending the triduum. It gets lonelier every year—fewer friends. Once Simon Elmes used to make a house party of it. Now I am alone with the new, impoverished liturgy" (British Library [BL], Add. MS 69798, fols. 37, 38). Waugh's diary entry for Easter 1956 reads: "I went to Downside on the Wednesday of Holy Week and stayed until after the High Mass of Easter. There were no friends staying at the monastery this year so that the triduum was without distraction. It was indeed rather boring since the new liturgy introduced for the first time this year leaves many hours unemployed. . . . I found myself . . . resentful of the new liturgy. On Thursday, instead of the morning Mass, mandatum, tenebrae and night vigil at the altar of repose, there was an afternoon Mass with the mandatum interpolated after the gospel and the altar of repose emptied at midnight. On Friday, instead of the Mass of the Presanctified, stations of the cross and tenebrae, an afternoon adoration of the cross and general communion. On Saturday nothing (except the conferences) all day until the Easter vigil at 10.30 in the same form we had suffered the last two years. . . . In spite of all I found the triduum valuable" (*The Diaries of Evelyn Waugh*, ed. Michael Davie [Weidenfeld and Nicolson, 1976], p. 758 [henceforth cited as Davie, *Diaries*]).

dioceses such as some in Asia and Africa, where half a dozen or more different tongues are spoken, translation is almost impossible. Even in England and the United States where much the same language is spoken by all, the difficulties are huge. There are colloquialisms which, though intelligible enough, are barbarous and absurd. The vernacular used may either be precise and prosaic, in which case it has the stilted manner of a civil servant's correspondence, or poetic and euphonious, in which case it will tend towards the archaic and less intelligible. The Authorised Version of the Bible of James I was not written in the current tongue but in that of a century earlier. Mgr Knox, a master of language, attempted in his translation of the Vulgate to devise a "timeless English", but his achievement has not been universally welcomed. I think it highly doubtful whether the average churchgoer either needs or desires to have complete intellectual, verbal comprehension of all that is said. He has come to worship, often dumbly and effectively. In most of the historic Churches the act of consecration takes place behind curtains or doors. The idea of crowding round the priest and watching all he does is quite alien there. It cannot be pure coincidence that so many independent bodies should all have evolved in just the same way. Awe is the natural predisposition to prayer. When young theologians talk, as they do, of Holy Communion as a "social meal" they find little response in the hearts and minds of their less sophisticated brothers.

No doubt there are certain clerical minds to whom the behaviour of the laity at Mass seems shockingly unregimented. We are assembled in obedience to the law of the Church. The priest performs his function in exact conformity to rule. But we—what are we up to? Some of us are following the missal, turning the pages adroitly to introits and extra collects, silently speaking all that the liturgists would like us to utter aloud and in unison. Some are saying the rosary. Some are wrestling with refractory children. Some are rapt in prayer. Some are thinking of all manner of irrelevant things until intermittently called to attention by the bell. There is no apparent "togetherness". Only in heaven are we recognisable as the united body we are. It is easy to see why some clergy would like us to show more consciousness of one another, more evidence of taking part in a social "group activity". Ideally they are right but that is to presuppose a very much deeper spiritual life in private than most of us have achieved.

If, like monks and nuns, we rose from long hours of meditation and solitary prayer for an occasional excursion into social solidarity in the public recitation of the office, we should, unquestionably, be leading the full Christian life to which we are dedicated. But that is not the case. Most of us, I think, are rather perfunctory and curt in our morning and evening prayers. The time we spend in Church—little enough—is what we set aside for renewing in our various ways our neglected contacts with God. It is not how it should be, but it is, I think, how it has always been for the majority of us and the Church in wisdom and charity has always taken care of the second-rate. If the Mass is changed in form so as to emphasise its social character, many souls will find themselves put at a further distance from their true aim. The danger is that the Conciliar Fathers, because of their own deeper piety and because they have been led to think that there is a strong wish for change on the part of the laity, may advise changes that will prove frustrating to the less pious and the less vocal.

It may seem absurd to speak of "dangers" in the Council when all Catholics believe that whatever is decided in the Vatican will be the will of God. It is the sacramental character of the Church that supernatural ends are attained by human means. The interrelation of the spiritual and material is the essence of the Incarnation. To compare small things with great, an artist's "inspiration" is not a process of passive acceptance of dictation. At work he makes false starts and is constrained to begin again; he feels impelled in one direction, happily follows it until he is conscious that he is diverging from his proper course; new discoveries come to him while he is toiling at some other problem, so that eventually by trial and error a work of art is consummated. So with the inspired decisions of the Church. They are not revealed by a sudden clear voice from heaven. Human arguments are the means by which the truth eventually emerges. It is not really impertinent to insinuate one more human argument into the lofty deliberations.

Archbishop Heenan
to Evelyn Waugh*

Venerabile Collegio Inglese
Via Monserrato 45, Rome

25 November 1962

Venerabilis Frater—as we say in the Council—I was delighted to see your article. There is nothing in there with which I don't agree. But what a pity the voice of the laity was not heard sooner. The enthusiasts who write in *The Tablet* and *Catholic Herald* are so easily mistaken for the intelligent and alive Catholics.

The real difficulty (I think) is that Continentals are twisting themselves inside out to make us look as like as possible to the Protestants. How I wish we could persuade them (a large majority I fear) that to be at home with our Mass and ceremonies is far more important than being right according to the books of liturgical antiquities.

In my Cathedral, by the way, nobody will be looking in anybody else's face (except perhaps, surreptitiously, two young lovers). The High altar is off centre and there will be no people behind it. The road will

*BL: Letters from Heenan to Waugh come from Waugh's uncatalogued incoming correspondence.

be clear for priests to bring the Blessed Sacrament at the Communion of the Mass.

God bless you.

+ John C Heenan
Archbishop of Liverpool.[1]

---

[1] The manuscript is annotated, "He went back on all this." Martin Stannard attributes this to Christopher Sykes (*Evelyn Waugh: No Abiding City, 1939–1966* [Dent, 1992], p. 480). Waugh also received a congratulatory letter from the bishop of Leeds, George Patrick O'Dwyer, dated 27 November 1962, which says: "'Optime! Optime!' as we Conciliar Latinists say. But why oh why didn't you write it twelve months ago in the Catholic press so that the inarticulate faithful could be encouraged to roar in support against the articulate few who want to dragoon every unfortunate congregation into a P.S.A. service? I did my best in the Council with an amendment to keep the damage to the pre-offertory part of the Mass and on Sundays only [intervention, 30 October 1962]. This a concession for the poor priests behind the Iron Curtain who are allowed neither to preach or teach but can still say Mass. Thus with the vernacular in the Mass of Catechumens they will be able to put some Christian doctrine to the people. I'm pretty confident we shan't have to suffer too much change. As for the Sacraments—the thought of some cleric pouring out his soul in the vernacular whilst administering Extreme Unction adds a formerly unknown terror to death" (BL). Waugh replied to Dwyer on 7 December 1962, adding: "Our congregation at Taunton has many refugees and Italian immigrants who will not feel more at home with English devotions" (Birmingham Archdiocesan Archives, GPD/E/E/34).

Evelyn Waugh to Lady Daphne Acton*

Combe Florey House

15 March 1963

Dearest Daphne,

I am returning the tract[1] you kindly lent me with some very cross marginalia. I didn't like it at all. Apart from objecting to much of the theme, I thought it common and cocksure in expression, sometimes asserting as fact what it had to prove and sometimes lapsing into commonplace.

Some people, like Penelope Betjeman, like making a row in church and I don't see why they shouldn't; just as the Abyssinians dance and wave rattles. I should feel jolly shy dancing and I feel shy praying out loud. Every parish might have one rowdy Mass a Sunday for those who like it. But there should be silent ones for those who like quiet.

The Uniate Churches are highly relevant. They are allowed to keep their ancient habits of devotion and to have a ritual in languages like Syriac, Byzantine

---

* *The Letters of Evelyn Waugh*, ed. Mark Amory (Weidenfeld and Nicolson, 1980), pp. 602–3 (henceforth cited as Amory, *Letters*).

[1] Presumably by Father (Charles) Davis, mentioned later in the letter, author of *Liturgy and Doctrine* (Sheed and Ward, 1960).

44

Greek, Ghiz [*sic*], Slavonic which are much deader than Latin. Why should we not have a Uniate Roman Church and let the Germans have their own knock-about performances?

I think it a great cheek of the Germans to try and teach the rest of the world anything about religion. They should be in perpetual sackcloth and ashes for all their enormities from Luther to Hitler.

The worst mistake of your Fr Davis is his almost blasphemous degradation of the conception of the Mystical Body into a parish meeting. You and I and the dancing Abyssinians and the saints in glory are, as you well know, integral parts of the Mystical Body. We don't have to be shouting one another down in the next pew.

When Fr Davis says that the new, impoverished Holy Week is a good thing because it teaches people the Old Testament, he is raving. There was six times as much Old Testament in the old services than the new.

The word "vernacular" is almost meaningless. If they intend to have versions of the liturgy in the everyday speech of everyone, they will have to have some hundreds of thousands of versions. In civilised countries Norway has two languages, Spain three, Milanese can't understand Sicilian etc. When you get to Asia and Africa it is Babel. As you know most African languages are quite incapable of conveying theological meanings and some haven't even a word for "virgin" I am told—simply two words for girls before and after puberty.

I have had a great scolding from Penelope Betjeman about my article.[2] She admits she just wants to make a noise—also to teach half-baked children.

Surely it is one of the signs of the Holy Ghost that the half-baked and illiterate do somehow grasp the truths of the Church without understanding the words?

The decision actually taken at the Council, I gather, will be that all the introduction to the canon of the Mass will be in the vernacular on days of obligation. They also say that we must have the same version as the Americans, heaven help us. . . .

Love from
Evelyn.

---

[2] "The Same Again, Please" (see pp. 27–41).

Evelyn Waugh—
Letter to the Editor of *The Tablet**

Sir,—The Eastern Uniate Churches retain ancient habits of worship which are dear to them, and liturgies which in many cases are unintelligible to the faithful. Is this not the time to seek similar privileges for Roman Catholics? Will you promote an appeal to the Holy See for the establishment of a Uniate Latin Church which shall observe all the rites as they existed in the reign of Pius IX?

> Your obedient servant,
> Evelyn Waugh.

* 16 March 1963.

Archbishop Heenan—
Pastoral Letter on the Vatican Council, Lent 1964

John Carmel, by the Grace of God and favour of the Apostolic See, Archbishop of Westminster and Metropolitan, to the Clergy and Faithful of the Diocese, health and blessing in the Lord.

Dearly Beloved Brethren and Dear Children in Jesus Christ:

Never before has the Church attracted such sympathy and interest in this country. Pick up your paper and every day you see some news item affecting Catholics. But you mustn't believe all you read. You have to be on your guard especially about reports from abroad. Look at the Council. Some papers gave splendid accounts but others reported only disagreements among the Council Fathers. There were, of course, disagreements and sometimes bishops spoke with heat. But that should surprise nobody. You would expect pastors of souls to feel strongly on questions affecting the salvation of souls.

The faithful also feel strongly about these questions. I know that from your letters. Take, for example, changes in Holy Mass. Some of you are quite alarmed. You imagine that everything will be changed and what you have known from childhood will be taken away from you. Some, on the other hand, are all for change and are afraid that too little will be altered.

Both these attitudes are wrong. The Church will, of course, make certain reforms. That is one of the reasons why Councils are held. But nothing will be changed except for the good of souls. With the Pope we bishops are the Teaching Church. We love our Faith and we love our priests and people. We shall see that you are not robbed. Loyal to Pope John and Pope Paul, the Council will bring all in the Church closer to Christ, and the world itself closer to the Church of Christ.

The Church believes in freedom and while a Council is in progress all are encouraged to speak freely. It is a time for priests and people to make their voices heard. Some of the views expressed are, of course, extraordinary. A few Catholic writers criticise so bitterly that you might think they forget that the Church is their mother. But at heart they really do love the Church. Perhaps they exaggerate to draw attention to their views. But they might easily mislead you. So let me tell you plainly that the Church has no power to alter the law of God. What is wrong and immoral can never become right. Nor can any doctrine of the Catholic Church be changed. "The truth of the Lord remaineth for ever" (Ps. 116, 2). I want to reassure you, my dear children in Jesus Christ. The Church, the Kingdom of God upon earth, is founded upon a rock. It will not fail you. For your consolation I repeat the words of Our Lord: "Fear not, little flock, for it

hath pleased your Father to give you a kingdom" (Luke
12, 32).

The Church will emerge from the Council stronger
than ever. We must prepare ourselves to be worthy of
that great hour. More and more people are asking about
the Church. You must be ready to answer their questions. Read your Catholic papers and the pamphlets
of the Catholic Truth Society. Show your love for our
separated brethren by giving them the information they
want. Fight bigotry and intolerance with all your
strength.

Today I ask your prayers for our Holy Father and
for the Council. During Lent try to attend Mass and
receive Holy Communion daily. Evening Mass and the
new rules for fasting make that possible for nearly everyone. When I go to Rome in a few days time I want to
be able to tell Pope Paul that the archdiocese will spend
Lent praying for him and the Council.

During Lent you will, I know, give up some luxury
to save money for those in need. There is distress all
around us despite the prosperity of our country. Old
people have inadequate pensions, widows with young
children face a daily struggle. If they work to help themselves and their families they will probably have their
allowances reduced. It sounds absurd—but that is the
present law. With Lenten alms I hope that we shall be
able to help such as these. As good citizens Catholics
should press politicians to hasten measures to bring relief
to the old, the bereaved and the homeless. For we must
not forget how many couples starting family life are in
desperation because of the housing shortage.

I end by begging your prayers and wishing you God's blessing. With St Paul I say: "Walk worthy of the vocation in which you are called" (Ephesians 4, 1). Let this Lent be a time of prayer and penance in the spirit of Paul the pilgrim Pope.

Given at Westminster on the 2nd day of February, the Feast of Our Lady's Purification, in the year of Our Lord nineteen hundred and sixty four, and appointed to be read at every Mass, morning and evening, in all the churches and chapels of the Archdiocese on Quinquagesima Sunday.[1]

+ John Carmel
Archbishop of Westminster.

[1] 9 February 1964.

Evelyn Waugh—
Diary Entry, Easter 1964*

Compare the Mass to the hunting-field. The huntsman's (priest's) primary task is to find and kill foxes. He is paid for this if he shows good sport to the followers. Some keep up with hounds if they are well mounted and know the country, and are in at the death; others coffee house [?] at coverts and trot about lanes.

When I first came into the Church I was drawn, not by splendid ceremonies but by the spectacle of the priest as a craftsman. He had an important job to do which none but he was qualified for. He and his apprentice stumped up to the altar with their tools and set to work without a glance to those behind them, still less with any intention to make a personal impression on them.

"Participate"—the cant word—does not mean to make a row as the Germans suppose. One participates in a work of art when one studies it with reverence and understanding.

* Davie, *Diaries*, pp. 792–93. In a letter to Ann Fleming dated 3 March 1964, Waugh wrote: "I go to Rome for Easter to avoid the horrors of the English Liturgy" (Amory, *Letters*, p. 618).

Evelyn Waugh—
Letter to the Editor of *The Times**

Sir,—Though an imperfect Latinist, I am in full sympathy with the regrets expressed by Mr Edward Hutton in his letter of today.[1] I think, however, that he exaggerates when he speaks of the proposed innovations as "splitting the Roman Catholic Church in England from top to bottom". The effect is more likely to be that church-going will become irksome but still a duty we shall all perform.

I think we can trust our bishops to mitigate the annoyance and distress. They have, I understand, considerable freedom of choice in the matter.

> I am, Sir, your obedient servant,
> Evelyn Waugh.

---

* 6 August 1964, published 8 August.

[1] Hutton's letter reacted to the announcement that English would be adopted "as the language of the Mass or part of it" in England and asked: "Would it not be possible to allow a Latin Mass to be said on Sundays at a convenient hour for those wedded to time-honoured ways?"

Evelyn Waugh—
Letter to the Editor of
*The Catholic Herald**

Sir,—Like all editors you justly claim that you are not responsible for the opinions of your correspondents and claim credit for establishing an open "forum". On the other hand you write of "exploding renewal" and "manifest dynamism of the Holy Spirit", thus seeming to sympathise with the northern innovators who wish to change the outward aspect of the Church. I think you injure your cause when week by week you publish (to me) fatuous and outrageous proposals by irresponsible people.

Father John Sheerin is neither fatuous nor outrageous but I find him a little smug. If I read him correctly he is pleading for magnanimity towards defeated opponents. The old (and young) buffers should not be reprobated. They have been imperfectly "instructed". The "progressive" should ask the "conservative with consummate courtesy" to re-examine his position.

I cannot claim consummate courtesy but may I, with round politeness, suggest that the progressives should re-examine their own? Were *they* perfectly instructed? Did they find the discipline of their seminaries rather

*7 August 1964.

irksome? Did they think they were wasting time on the Latin which they found uncongenial? Do they want to marry and beget other little progressives? Do they, like the present Pope, think Italian literature a more enjoyable pursuit than apologetics?

The distinction between Catholicism and *Romanità* has already been stressed in the American journal *Commonweal*. Of course it is possible to have Faith without *Romanità* and to have *Romanità* without the Faith, but as a matter of recorded history the two have kept very close. "Peter has spoken" remains the guarantee of orthodoxy.

It is surely (?) a journalistic trick to write of "the Johannine era". Pope John was a pious and attractive man. Many of the innovations, which many of us find so obnoxious, were introduced by Pius XII.[1] Pope John's life at Bergamo, Rome, in the Levant, at Paris and Venice was lived with very meagre association with Protestants until, in his extreme old age, he found himself visited by polite clergymen of various sects whom he greeted, as he did the Russian atheists, with "consummate courtesy".

I do not believe he had any conception of the true character of modern Protestantism. I quote from an article in *Time* magazine of 10 July:

> The one persuasive way of referring to Jesus today is as a "remarkably free man". After the Resurrection the disciples suddenly possessed some of the unique

---

[1] Waugh is referring in particular to the reform of Holy Week carried out under Pius XII: see pp. 36–38 above.

and "contagious" freedom that Jesus had. In telling
the story of Jesus of Nazareth, therefore, they told it
as the story of the free man who had set them free. . . .
He who says "Jesus is love" says that Jesus' freedom
has been contagious. . . . Van Buren concludes that
Christianity will have to strip itself of its supernatural elements . . . just as alchemy had to abandon its
mystical overtones to become the useful science of
Chemistry.

These words are not the words of a Californian crank
but of a clergyman of the "Episcopal Church" of America, who derive what Orders they have from the Archbishop of Canterbury. I am sure that such questions
were not raised on the much-publicised meeting of
the Archbishop and Pope John.

Father Sheerin suggests that Catholic conservatism
is the product of the defensive policy necessary in
the last century against the nationalistic-masonic secu-
larism of the time. I would ask him to consider that
the function of the Church in every age has been
conservative—to transmit undiminished and uncon-
taminated the creed inherited from its predecessors.
Not "is this fashionable notion one that we should
accept?" but "is this dogma (a subject on which we
agree) the Faith as we received it?" has been the question (as far as I know) at all General Councils. I have
seen no evidence that Pope Paul [sic] had anything
else in mind when he summoned the present Council.

Conservatism is not a new influence in the Church.
It is not the heresies of the sixteenth and seventeenth
centuries, the agnosticism of the eighteenth century,

the atheism of the nineteenth and twentieth centuries, that have been the foes of the Faith turning her from serene supremacy to sharp controversy. Throughout her entire life the Church has been at active war with enemies from without and traitors from within. The war against Communism in our own age is acute but it is mild compared with those fought and often won by our predecessors.

Finally, a word about liturgy. It is natural to the Germans to make a row. The torchlit, vociferous assemblies of the Hitler Youth expressed a national passion. It is well that this should be canalized into the life of the Church. But it is essentially un-English. We seek no "Sieg Heils". We pray in silence. "Participation" in the Mass does not mean hearing our own voices. It means God hearing our voices. Only He knows who is "participating" at Mass. I believe, to compare small things with great, that I "participate" in a work of art when I study it and love it silently. No need to shout. Anyone who has taken part in a play knows that he can rant on the stage with his mind elsewhere. If the Germans want to be noisy, let them. But why should they disturb our devotions?

"Diversity" is deemed by the progressives as one of their aims against the stifling *Romanità*. May they allow it to English Catholics.

I am now old but I was young when I was received into the Church. I was not at all attracted by the splendour of her great ceremonies—which the Protestants could well counterfeit. Of the extraneous attractions of the Church which most drew me was the spectacle of the priest and his server at low Mass, stumping up to the altar without a glance to discover how many or how few he had in his congregation; a craftsman and his apprentice; a man with a job which he alone was qualified to do. That is the Mass I have grown to know and love. By all means let the rowdy have their "dialogues", but let us who value silence not be completely forgotten.

Your obedient servant,
Evelyn Waugh.

Evelyn Waugh to
Archbishop Heenan*

Combe Florey House

16 August 1964

My Dear Archbishop,

Please forgive my presumption in sending you the enclosed press cutting. I do so with no belief in its intrinsic interest. You must be tediously familiar with all that it says. I send it because I have been greatly surprised by the consequences. I wrote it last week to *The Catholic Herald*, a paper mainly written and read by the fervent "progressives". I have received a large post the burden of which was 'Why do not you (I) do something to lead a party? Why not organise a petition to the Archbishop?'

I do not think a petition would impress you. It is notorious that one can collect signatures for any cause if one takes the trouble. But I do wonder whether the hierarchy are fully aware of the distress caused by their Advent threat—not so much by the modest and reasonable innovations proposed but by the opening it seems to offer to more radical and distasteful changes.

* AAW, HE 1/142.

I think I owe it to my very numerous correspondents to put their case to you. A few were priests, mostly laymen and laywomen of middle or old age; about half, I conjecture, converts who ask: 'Why were we led out of the church of our childhood to find the church of our adoption assuming the very forms we disliked?'

Is it too much to ask that all parishes should be ordered to have two Masses, a "Pop" for the young and a "Trad" for the old? I think that a vociferous minority has imposed itself on the hierarchy and made them believe that a popular demand existed where there was in fact not even a preference.

My trade is in words and I daily become more sceptical about verbal comprehension—especially in the odd hinterland of verbal prayers.

Pray forgive my impertinence in advising you, who have far wider sources of information than I.

> Yours sincerely,
> Evelyn Waugh.

Archbishop Heenan to
Evelyn Waugh*

Hare Street House
Buntingford, Herts.

20 August 1964

My Dear Mr Waugh,

I had read and enjoyed your letter to the Catholic Herald. My first reaction was gratitude that you had written. People may call you reactionary but nobody can call you a fool. I think that the leaders of the new thought (if that is not too strong a word) are not so much the young pops as the Catholic "intellectuals". This is what they call themselves and believe themselves to be. Everyone with two A levels is now an intellectual.

These are the people who complain about the cleavage between the hierarchy and the educated laity: and who largely create it. They regard us as mitred peasants and look for guidance to the continental clergy (who have so largely been abandoned by the workers) or to their former schoolmasters (who naturally lack pastoral experience).

*BL.

The hierarchy is in a difficult position. We have not yet lost the respect of ordinary Catholics but the constant nagging of the intellectuals and their tireless (tiresome?) letters to the Press and articles in the Catholic papers may eventually disturb the ordinary faithful. Most of us would be content to delay changes but the mood of the Council compels us to act. Otherwise the attack from our own people would become ever more bitter: *inimici hominis domestici scies.*

But do not despair. The changes are not so great as they are made to appear. Although a date has been set for introducing the new liturgy I shall be surprised if all of the bishops will want *all* Masses every day to be in the new rite. We shall try to keep the needs of *all* in mind—Pops, Trads, Rockers, Mods, With-its, and Without-its.

I hope you will dine with me if you ever come to London.

God bless you and your family.

> + John Carmel
> Archbishop of Westminster.

Evelyn Waugh to Archbishop Heenan*

Combe Florey House

25 August 1964

Dear Archbishop,

Very many thanks for your kind letter. I have no wish to add to your burdens by drawing you into a correspondence, but literally every day I get letters from distressed laymen who think I might speak for them.

The distress is not caused by the modest changes in the Mass threatened in Advent but by the tone of the "progressives" who seem to regard these as a mere beginning of radical changes.

I detect a new kind of anticlericalism. The old anticlericals, by imputing avarice, ambition, immorality etc. to the priesthood at least recognised its peculiar and essential character, which made lapses notable. The new anticlericals seem to minimise the sacramental character of the priesthood and to suggest that the laity are their equals.

It is most kind of you to suggest a meeting. It would be a great pleasure to me. I am engaged on Sept. 3rd.

* AAW, HE 1/142.

Apart from that evening I could come to London at any time. You must have a full engagement book. Have you any evening before the end of September when you could dine with me alone and incognito at my London club?

Yours sincerely,
Evelyn Waugh.

Archbishop Heenan to Evelyn Waugh*

Archbishop's House
Westminster, London SW1

28 August 1964

My dear Mr Waugh,

Of course you are right. That is why they are playing up this People of God and Priesthood of the Laity so much. The Mass is no longer the Holy Sacrifice but the Meal at which the priest is the waiter. The bishop, I suppose, is the head waiter and the Pope the Patron.

We shall talk more of this. I return to London on Friday next and leave for Rome on 13th Sept. I am away from diaries but will you ask someone to ring my secretary (Mgr Kent or Fr Burke) Victoria 4717 and arrange to come to dinner on 8th, 9th or 10th Sept. Come early, about 7 o'clock. I shall not invite anyone else.

> Devotedly,
>
> + John Carmel
> Archbishop of Westminster.

*BL.

Evelyn Waugh to
Katharine Asquith*

Combe Florey House

14 September 1964

Dearest Katharine,

... I was shanghaied from the train on Friday by Violet Powell & spent the night at Chantry. It was tantalising to be so near and not to see you. I had been summoned to London to dine tête-à-tête with Archbishop Heenan to discuss the attitude of the laity to the liturgical innovations. He showed himself as deeply conservative and sympathetic to those of us who are scared of the new movement. He thinks that "the intellectuals" are all against him. "They regard us as mitred peasants", he said. I think I was able to encourage him a little. . . .

Love to Helen.
Evelyn.

* Amory, *Letters*, p. 624.

Evelyn Waugh to
Lady Diana Cooper*

Combe Florey House

All Saints' 1964

Darling Pug,

... The Vatican Council weighs heavily on my spirits. Truth will prevail I have no doubt but a great deal of balls is being talked. ...

All love,
Bo.

*BL Add. MS 69798, fol. 70.

Evelyn Waugh to
Lady Diana Cooper*

Combe Florey House

7th February 1965

Darling,

... Nice to go to Rome. They are destroying all that was superficially attractive about my Church. It is a great sorrow to me and for once undeserved. If you see Cardinal Bea spit in his eye.

All love,
Bo.

* BL Add. MS 69798, fol. 73.

Evelyn Waugh to
Archbishop Heenan*

Combe Florey House

3 January 1965

Dear Archbishop,

Please forgive me for troubling you. I read in many papers that the clergy welcome advice from the laity. I doubt if this is true, but your kindness at our last meeting emboldens me to write. You sent me away reassured that the novelties about to be introduced would be much mitigated. I do not know how things are in Westminster. In the provinces they are *tohu bohu* (if you will forgive a quotation from a language otherwise unknown to me).

Apart from the distress at finding our spiritual habits disordered (and I know this is a minor concern compared with the graver dangers to faith and morals openly propounded at the Council) my friends and I are totally at a loss to understand the new form of the Mass.

Any idea that it will attract Protestants may be dismissed. The Anglicans have an elegant and

* AAW, HE 1/142.

comprehensible form of service. All they lack is valid orders to make it preferable. If a completely English Mass is desired the first book of Edward VI, with very few amendments, would be satisfactory. Instead we have a jumble of Greek, Latin and uncouth English.

In the old Mass a glance at the altar was enough to inform me of the precise stage of the liturgy. The priest's voice was often inaudible and unintelligible. I do not write with the pride of a classical scholar. Indeed I know less Latin now than I did 45 years ago. But it did not require any high state of prayer to unite oneself to the action of the priest.

Repeatedly standing up and saying "And with you" detracts from this relatively intimate association and "participation".

Certain parts of the Mass were familiar to the least educated eg. the *Pater Noster*, the *Credo*, *Domine non sum dignus* etc. These only have been put into English.

Why are we constantly badgered to subscribe to Catholic schools if they are unable to impart these rudiments?

Why is *Corpus Christi* translated? Are we in future to have "Body of Christ processions"?

Why are we deprived of the prayers at communion, which even the Anglicans retain: *custodiat animam tuam in vitam æternam*?

I have lately heard a sermon (not of course from the admirable Canon Iles[1]) where we were told that we had no business at Mass unless we received communion unless we are in mortal sin.

---

[1] The parish priest of Taunton.

Martindale and Knox are dead. There may be young preachers. I have not had the good fortune to hear them. Why all these sermons when here and abroad a large proportion of the congregation is foreign?

Why is the *Agnus Dei* first in Latin, then in English?

Why does the priest recite the creed, which we all know, from the pulpit?

Every attendance at Mass leaves me without comfort or edification. I shall never, pray God, apostatize but church-going is now a bitter trial.

Presumably in Low Week you and your fellow bishops will discuss the effects of the "experiments". Please tell them how much distress they cause and please pray for my perseverance.

Yours very sincerely,
Evelyn Waugh.

Archbishop Heenan to Evelyn Waugh*

Archbishop's House
Westminster, London SW1

17 January 1965

Carissime,

Alas! After three months' absence I have been quite unable to catch up with correspondence awaiting me: much less deal with what the Americans call incoming mail. Forgive me.

You may have seen that I have told each parish priest to call a meeting to seek views and reactions from the faithful. At present the Mass is an untidy mess.

I have called a meeting of bishops for next month. There are so many things which, I agree with you, are undesirable. But the *vast* majority (my priests tell me) enjoys the English in the Mass: even many who were opposed before.

With an affectionate blessing and hoping to see you again soon.

Devotedly,

+ John C Heenan
Archbishop of Westminster.

*BL.

Cardinal Heenan—Pastoral Letter on the Vatican Council, Lent 1965

John Carmel, Cardinal Priest of the Holy Roman Church of the title of San Silvestro in Capite, by the Grace of God and favour of the Apostolic See, Archbishop of Westminster and Metropolitan, to the Clergy and Faithful of the Diocese, health and blessing in the Lord.

Dearly Beloved Brethren and Dear Children in Jesus Christ:

The Council will soon be over. The date of the fourth and final session has been announced by the Pope. Probably there will not be another Council in your lifetime or in mine. So it is worth discussing once again.

Hard things have been said about this Second Vatican Council. Some go so far as to say that they heartily wish it had never taken place. They have been disturbed by the criticisms of the Church made by her own children. They suspect that some Catholics, mistaking the nature of ecumenism, are seeking to water down the truths of Faith—especially those relating to the Holy Sacrifice of the Mass and the Mother of God. Converts complain, not without bitterness, that what attracted them to the Church is now being taken away. They have in mind the spiritual security given by the voice of a Church speaking with authority.

There can be no doubt that this distress of mind and soul is genuine. It is important, therefore, to try to see what the Council is likely to achieve. Pope John, it is true, did not foresee when he summoned the Council that it would last so long. He was later to regret the long absences of bishops from their flocks. He also grieved over what was said or written to alarm and discourage faithful Catholics. But he never doubted that the Council is the work of God. He was convinced that the time had come for the Church to look closely at herself; to discover if any reform was needed; and to seek new ways of bringing the message of Christ to the world. No Pope did more than he to heal the wounds of a divided Christendom. The Council was his chosen instrument to renovate the Church and to foster Christian Unity.

We must not pretend that nothing needed to be changed. Truth itself does not alter but knowledge of the truth is always changing—otherwise there could never be any development of Christian doctrine. Customs also change. Look, for example, at the alterations in the length of the Eucharistic fast. Once the fast was from midnight. Then it was reduced to three hours. Now the Church requires us to fast only for one hour and, as a result, hundreds of thousands receive Holy Communion more frequently.

The changes in the Mass have made the greatest impact on the faithful. Some complain that the use of English in the Mass has meant throwing away the benefits of a universal language in a universal Church. It is true that something is lost by having an English liturgy. But the Pope and the bishops of the whole Church were convinced that it would be an immense gain to the majority of the faithful if their mother tongue were used. Whatever be our personal preferences, the fact is that millions who hitherto were mere bystanders are now taking an active part in the Mass.

The Council has brought changes and to many Catholics these changes are painful. But change is almost always painful. Slum clearance, for example, which compels old people to exchange squalor for clean decency is often at first resisted. So with the Council. There is much to cause discomfort. Controversy is in the air and every man tends to become his own theologian. Startling opinions are frequently expressed. But this proves what Catholics have always contended—that liberty exists in the Church. During a Council there are bound to be those, striving to be in the fashion of thought, who will cause scandal. But these fashions will soon pass. Next year not the speeches and articles but the decisions of the Church will matter. And in making decisions the Council is guided by the Holy Spirit of God.

Let this Lent be a season of fervent prayer and self-denial. Offer daily Mass and Holy Communion that God will guide the bishops and theologians in the Council to speak and act with wisdom and prudence. The Council is not a public meeting of bishops. It is the Church of God assembled to hear His voice and obey His Will. This Council is your Council. Thank God for it and beg His blessing on His Holy Church.

Given at Westminster on the twenty-seventh day of Febru-ary, the Feast of St Gabriel of Our Lady of Sorrows, in the year of Our Lord nineteen hundred and sixty five, and appointed to be read at every Mass, morning and evening, in all the churches and chapels of the Archdiocese on Quin-quagesima Sunday.[1]

+ John Cardinal Heenan
Archbishop of Westminster

[1] 28 February 1965.

Evelyn Waugh to
Monsignor McReavy*

Combe Florey House

15 April 1965[1]

Rt Rev Monsignor,

Pray forgive me for troubling you. I do so because I am told you are often kind enough to give expert advice to troubled laymen.

When I was instructed in the faith some 35 years ago I was told of the obligation to hear mass on the appointed days (a) that it applied only to those living within three miles of a church and that the invention of the motor-car had not modified this ruling and (b) that the obligation applied only from the Offertory to the Priest's Communion.

Is this still the law?

I do not ask what is best for me; merely what is the least I am obliged to do without grave sin. I find the

---

* Amory, *Letters*, pp. 630–31. Monsignor McReavy answered queries in the *Clergy Review*.

[1] Maundy Thursday.

new liturgy a temptation against Faith, Hope and Charity but I shall never, pray God, apostatize.

I enclose an envelope for your kind reply.[2]

Your obedient servant,
E. Waugh.

[2] Amory indicates that the reply stated that Waugh was technically correct on the first point but that the obligation referred to the whole Mass.

Evelyn Waugh—Diary Entry,
Easter 1965*

A year in which the process of transforming the liturgy has followed a planned course. Protests avail nothing. A minority of cranks, for and against the innovations, mind enormously. I don't think the main congregation cares a hoot.

More than the aesthetic changes which rob the Church of poetry, mystery and dignity, there are suggested changes in Faith and morals which alarm me. A kind of anti-clericalism is abroad which seeks to reduce the priest's unique sacramental position. The Mass is written of as a "social meal" in which the "people of God" perform the consecration.

Pray God I will never apostatize but I can only now go to church as an act of duty and obedience—just as a sentry at Buck House[1] is posted with no possibility of his being employed to defend the sovereign's life.

Cardinal Heenan has been double-faced in the matter. I had dinner with him *à deux* in which he expressed complete sympathy with the conservatives and, as I understood him, promised resistance to the

* Davie, *Diaries*, p. 793.
[1] Buckingham Palace.

innovations which he is now pressing forward. How does he suppose the cause of participation is furthered by the prohibition of kneeling at the *incarnatus* in the creed?

The Catholic Press has made no opposition. I shall not live to see things righted.

Evelyn Waugh—Letter to the Editor of *The Tablet**

Dear Sir,—The pundits explain the continuing process of change in the liturgy by saying that it helps the laity to 'participate' in the Mass.

Can they, please, explain how this desirable object is furthered by today's peremptory prohibition of kneeling at the *incarnatus* in the creed?

Your obedient servant,
Evelyn Waugh.

* 24 April 1965.

Evelyn Waugh—Letter to the Editor of *The Tablet**

Fides, quaerens, intellectum

Dear Sir,—A first reading of your article under the above title gave me the hope that at last you had spoken out for suffering Catholics who have for many years now seen their public devotions stripped of more and more which they valued. A second reading reveals this hope to be premature.[1] Study the history of the Church, you tell us, and we shall see that it has been constantly on the defensive against enemies from without and traitors from within. It has prevailed. Unless I misunderstand you, you say there is no need to worry. It is not for us to try and correct the manifest errors of the innovators. Complacently accede to whatever is being proposed.

You appeal to history. To history let us turn. You will find that there have been a few inspired geniuses who have revivified the Church and, in doing so, changed it. For every one of these there have been hundreds of presumptuous and misguided men whose ambitions have come to nothing: who

* 31 July 1965.
[1] *Tablet*, 17 July 1965, pp. 792–93.

82

have been silenced, imprisoned or executed. Most of these innovators have found support among some of the higher clergy. There is nothing new about the present dangers except the lassitude with which they are accepted. It seems to me smug to congratulate ourselves on the absence of *odium theologicum.*

You express a special solicitude for elderly converts. You may well do so for we are likely to be the last converts of the century, or longer.

You remark that the liturgical changes might have been more tactfully imposed, blandly assuming that the changes were necessary and desirable. Who in England wanted them?

I think the heart of the matter is: do you seek uniformity or diversity in the Church? On one hand the pundits say we must adapt our habits to the most exotic styles, taking off our boots instead of our hats in church in Asia, in Africa beating drums and dancing to express our devotion. In the Church of Christ the King, Oklahoma, the people instead of kneeling at the consecration and elevation of the host, crowd round the priest strumming guitars. All the tongues of Babel are to be employed save only Latin, the language of the Church since the mission of St Augustine. That is forbidden us. Why are we constantly asked to give money to schools if the children learn so little there that *Corpus Christi, Pater Noster, Domine, non sum dignus* are unintelligible to them?

We do not claim to impose our tastes and habits on those who find them unsympathetic. All we ask is that in every church where it is feasible there should be one Mass on every day of obligation said as in the days of good Pius IX.

Your obedient servant,
Evelyn Waugh.

Evelyn Waugh—Letter to the Editor of *The Tablet**

Dear Sir,—Brigadier Chamberlain may rest assured that for a long time representations have been made "quietly and unobtrusively through the proper channels" by those distressed at the changes in the Mass.[1] It was because these representations were disregarded that I urged you to make a public protest.

I agree with Mr Igoe that some Catholics prefer the vernacular and are entitled to it, though I cannot see how we are "raising up the mind and heart to God" by standing up and declaiming in unison: "And with you."[2] Certainly many cannot follow the Latin liturgy any more than an infant can understand the words which are spoken at his baptism. The flow of Grace is not impeded by vocabulary.

But language is merely a question of aesthetics. I detect graver dangers to the Faith, chief among them a lowering of respect for the unique office of the priesthood and episcopate in the talk of "the people of God" as consecrating the elements.

* 14 August 1965.
[1] See letter to the editor, *Tablet*, 7 August 1965, p. 889.
[2] See ibid., p. 888.

We have had the "liturgical movement" with us in parts of the USA and northern Europe for a generation. We looked on them as harmless cranks who were attempting to devise a charade of second-century habits. We had confidence in the abiding *Romanità* of our Church. Suddenly we find the cranks in authority.

In the sixteenth century the demand for Communion in both kinds (itself inoffensive) became a characteristic of heresy. In rather the same way today the appetite for small interpolations and abridgements, for raising the voice instead of the mind and heart, the disordering of services of great beauty and meaning which have developed through the centuries (e.g. the ritual of Good Friday) may prove to be symptoms of grave ill.

Pace Brigadier Chamberlain I think it is the duty of us all, and especially of you, sir, as editor of an influential paper, to warn the submissive laity of the dangers impending.

> I am, Sir, your obedient servant,
> Evelyn Waugh.

Evelyn Waugh—Letter to the Editor of *The Tablet**

Dear Sir,—I am sorry to baffle "Presbyter"; I gratefully return his salute.[1] My answer to both his questions is: yes. I should welcome the reimposition of the Eucharistic fast and the abolition of evening Masses. I think we are suffering from an extremity of the reaction against Jansenism and that Holy Communion is taken altogether too casually without, I suspect, in many cases, proper preparation and thanksgiving.

With regard to fasting in general, I must declare my interest. I have passed the age where it is obligatory. But I think it would not be intolerable in a world where a large part of the population is fasting through poverty and another large part is fasting through vanity, to the extent of paying up to £50 a week to starve in clinics.

---

* 21 August 1965.

[1] See letter to the editor, *Tablet*, 14 August 1965, p. 914. "Presbyter" asked "Mr Waugh and others who would have the Mass 'just as in the days of Pius IX'", "Would they also have the fasting laws as in the days of Pius IX—both the rigorous Lenten fast (with Sundays days of abstinence) and many other fasting days during the year, and also the eucharistic fast from midnight, which would mean, in effect, no evening Masses?"

If, as they claim, the liturgists wish to emulate the Church of the earliest centuries, would they not do well to fast rigorously?

A further point: when one considers the incomprehensibility of the *avant garde* in literature, drama and painting, is *aggiornamento* the right word for the innovations?

> Your obedient servant,
> Evelyn Waugh.

Evelyn Waugh—Letter to the Editor of *The Tablet**

Sir,—You recently published a letter from Mr Christopher Sykes in which he commented on increasing and exorbitant demands of the "liturgists", who use the smallest concession charitably made them to press for more radical and unseemly changes in the Mass.[1] You also, some time before, published a letter from myself warning you that the dangers threatening the Church were to be resisted on graver grounds than the merely sentimental, aesthetic or traditional.

A significant emphasis on our protests comes from the USA in the magazine *Commonweal*. The author is Fr John J. Ryan of the diocese of Peoria now, we are told, employed in writing "catechetical materials" in Chicago.

He begins by quoting a friendly priest who, with what he describes as "healthy irreverence", remarked: "Now that we have the liturgy in English, the people will really see how absurd it is."

The liturgy, he says, "fixed in all essentials" for the "tribal men" of late Roman society, says "next to nothing" about the "insights" of contemporary man. The

---

* 18 September 1965.
[1] See letter to the editor, *Tablet*, 21 August 1965, p. 938.

Gloria is a "curious thing". The Canon an "obscure and puzzling list of Roman worthies."

He goes on to object to the constant use of "we" and "us," to the humble pleading of our "wretchedness, helplessness, etc.," to expressions such as "divine teachings, divine mysteries, etc.," and to the aspiration that: "With you as ruler and guide we may pass through the good things of this world so as not to lose those of the world to come." Fr Ryan's insight tells him that "the things of this world are already, fundamentally, inchoately those of the world to come."

Fr Ryan wishes to change the words "low obedience, duty, virtue" (I presume he is here referring to his catechism) for "encounter, commitment and involvement."

He nowhere suggests the unique sanctity of the priestly office—a point I made in my previous letter to you. The priest must not emerge "like a God in an ancient pageant". Vestments are out and, also, it seems, any distinguishing costume. Instead he wishes to have a "priest-president" who will conduct a "sort of town meeting" to discuss social projects. The people would discuss their worries and share their "developing insights". The priest-president will sum up, giving the "ancient Eucharistic prayer a whole new tone and content."

There should be "improvisations, impromptu additions and substitutions in the liturgy . . . greater exchange and converse among the worshippers themselves, the priest-president acting as something of a chairman and commentator".

Those who are curious to follow Fr Ryan's catechetical ambitions at length may do so in *Commonweal*, August 20th. . . . Others may be content to accept
these few extracts as a warning of the underground
movement active almost everywhere in the Church
which is far from being a bogeyman imagined by the
traditionalists.

I am, Sir, your obedient servant,
Evelyn Waugh.

Cardinal Heenan to Evelyn Waugh*

Archbishop's House
Westminster, London SW1

12 January 1966

My dear Evelyn,

I rarely keep new year resolutions but I must keep this one—to write to you. I want to thank you for all that you have done for the Old Faith and to hope that you will be doing more in the coming year.

Recent years have been very trying but reflecting on the Council I am sure that it was a Good Thing. The last session brought sanity to the surface and I expect that before two years have passed we shall begin to reap results.

Do let me know when you are likely to be coming to London. I would so like to have you here for a nice anti-progressive dinner.

An affectionate blessing to the family.

+ John Card. Heenan

*BL.

Evelyn Waugh
to Cardinal Heenan*

Combe Florey House

14 January 1966

My Lord Cardinal,

Very many thanks for your kind letter which encourages me to cling to the Faith despite all that is being done to degrade it.

It is a joy that you are back amongst us and that the Council is over. I cannot hope that either of us will live to see its multitude of ills put right. The Church has endured and survived many dark periods. It is our misfortune to live in one of them.

Please pray for my perseverance and for that of the many English Catholics who are distressed and bewildered by the changes imposed on them.

I am fortunate enough to live midway between two admirable parishes. My brother-in-law has become an Orthodox Christian.

* AAW, HE I/142.

The assurances you gave me when you very kindly invited me to see you in London have been disappointed, but not as disastrously as the press made seem likely.

I am your eminence's obedient servant,
Evelyn Waugh.

Evelyn Waugh
to Lady Diana Mosley*

Combe Florey House

9 March 1966

Dearest Diana,

... I have become very old in the last two years. Not diseased but enfeebled. There is nowhere I want to go and nothing I want to do and I am conscious of being an utter bore. The Vatican Council has knocked the guts out of me. . . .

All love,
Evelyn.

*Amory, *Letters*, p. 638.

Evelyn Waugh to
Lady Diana Mosley*

Combe Florey House

30 March 1966

Dearest Diana,

... Easter used to mean so much to me. Before Pope
John and his Council—they destroyed the beauty of
the liturgy. I have not yet soaked myself in petrol and
gone up in flames, but I now cling to the Faith dog-
gedly without joy. Church-going is a pure duty parade.
I shall not live to see it restored. It is worse in many
countries. . . .

All love,
Evelyn.

* Amory, *Letters*, p. 639.

†

Evelyn Waugh
died
in his home
on Easter Sunday
10 April 1966
having returned from
morning Mass
celebrated in Latin
by Father Philip Caraman, S.J.

R.I.P.

Margaret Waugh to Lady Diana Cooper*

Combe Florey House

Easter Thursday[1]

Dear Lady Diana,

Don't be too upset about Papa. I think it was a kind of wonderful miracle. You know how he longed to die and dying as he did on Easter Sunday,[2] when all the liturgy is about death and resurrection, after a Latin Mass and holy communion would be exactly as he wanted. I am sure he had prayed for death at Mass. I am very, very happy for him.

He was talking of you a lot in the last few days. He had been upset and worried by your burglary. Also we talked a lot of our stay with you at Chantilly which was just ten years ago.

All my love,
Margaret.

Mummy loved your letter and I think will write later.

* BL, Add. MS 69798, fol. 117.
[1] 14 April 1966.
[2] 10 April 1966.

Laura Waugh to Lady Diana Cooper*

Combe Florey House[1]

Darling Diana,

Thank you so much for your letter. You meant so much to Evelyn and you do understand so well—I think he had been praying for death for a long time and it could not have happened more beautifully or happily for him—and without any physical suffering or illness—so I can only thank God for this mercy to Evelyn. But life will never be the same for us without him.

There is a memorial Mass for him on Thursday[2] at Westminster Cathedral but I shouldn't come as I know we have always hated the trappings of death. But do please say a prayer for him and for me.

All my love,
Laura.

---

* BL, Add. MS 69798, fol. 118.
[1] The manuscript has no date.
[2] 21 April 1966.

Panegyric

Father Philip Caraman, S.J.

Preached at the Latin requiem Mass celebrated by Monsignor George Tomlinson at Westminster Cathedral on 21st April 1966, in the presence of John Carmel Cardinal Heenan and of Archbishop Hyginus Cardinale, Apostolic Delegate.[1]

There was no man in England more entitled to give his opinion on the new English liturgy. Yet, when on the first Sunday Mass was said in English, he was asked about it, he answered instantly: "The question does not arise." Only when he was outraged beyond Christian endurance by manifest heresy, did he express himself in a letter to the press. The letter, I recall, touched on the Eucharist. He showed the anger Christ had when he cleansed the Temple.

It has been truthfully said by a Catholic friend that the tabernacle and the sanctuary lamp were for him the symbols of an unchanging Church in a crumbling society. There is a futuristic short story of his which describes how, after an atomic explosion in London, a man emerges and wanders about a dead and ruined city till he is drawn by the distant sound of a bell and, making his way into a cave below Piccadilly Circus,

[1] This extract contains Father Caraman's treatment of Waugh's liturgical views. The full text is published in the *Tablet*, 30 April 1966, p. 318.

sees a cluster of shawled women huddled round a priest as he offers Mass. When the priest turns round with a gesture and phrase the survivor recognizes, he is seen to have a black face.[2]

The Mass mattered for him most in his world. During the greater part of his lifetime it remained as it had done for centuries, the same and everywhere recognizable, when all else was threatened with change. He was sad when he read of churches in which the old altar was taken down and a table substituted, or of side altars abolished as private Masses were held to be unliturgical or unnecessary. With all who know something of the pattern of history, he was perturbed.

It was a struggle to accept it all, but he did accept it, and with enviable fidelity. The calmness that was evident in the last weeks of his life was a sign that the struggle had been won. To those who were with him on his final day—his family and a priest (he surely prayed for this)—nothing was more manifest than the way God had arranged his end as a mark of gratitude to a faithful servant.

I should be doing him the greatest disservice if I did not beg you all here to pray for him now: not only his friends who owe him this, but all who would make some return for the pleasure they have derived from his pen.

---

[2] See "Out of Depth" (1933), in *The Complete Stories of Evelyn Waugh* (Everyman's Library, 2000), pp. 135ff.

Cardinal Heenan—Intervention at the Synod of Bishops, Rome, October 1967

Like all the bishops I offer my sincere thanks to the Consilium. Its members have worked well and have done their best. I cannot help wondering, however, if the Consilium as at present constituted can meet the needs of our times? For the liturgy is not primarily an academic or cultural question. It is above all a pastoral matter for it concerns the spiritual lives of our faithful. I do not know the names of the members of the Consilium or, even more important, the names of their consultors. But after studying the so-called Normative Mass it was clear to me that few of them can have been parish priests. I cannot think that anyone with pastoral experience would have regarded the sung Mass as being of first importance.

At home it is not only women and children but also fathers of families and young men who come regularly to Mass. If we were to offer them the kind of ceremony we saw yesterday in the Sistine Chapel (a demonstration of the Normative Mass)[1] we would soon be left with a congregation of mostly women and children. Our people love the Mass but it is Low Mass

---

[1] 24 October 1967. A critique of Cardinal Heenan's intervention may be found in Annibale Bugnini, C.M., *The Reform of the Liturgy, 1948–1975* (Liturgical Press, 1990), pp. 348–50.

without psalm-singing and other musical embellishments to which they are chiefly attached. I humbly suggest that the Consilium look at its members and advisers to make sure that the number of those who live in seminaries and religious communities does not exceed the numbers of those with pastoral experience among the people in ordinary parishes.

Here are a few points which solely for the sake of time—since only five minutes are allowed for comments—must be put so shortly as to sound brusque.

1. The rule of prayer is the rule of faith. If there is to be more emphasis in the Mass on Bible readings than on Eucharistic prayer the faith of both clergy and people will be weakened.

2. There is more need than ever today to stress the Real Presence of our Lord in the Blessed Sacrament. No change in the Mass should be made which might seem to throw doubt on this doctrine.

3. Many bishops in this Synod have spoken of the need of coming to the rescue of the faithful grown restless and disturbed on account of too frequent changes in the Mass. I must therefore ask what attitude the Consilium will take to these warnings from the pastors of the Church? I confess in all seriousness that I am uneasy lest the liturgists say "These bishops know nothing about liturgy". It would be tragic if after the bishops have gone home no notice were to be taken of their opinions.

4. In my diocese of Westminster—and in several English dioceses—the rule is that at least one Mass

each Sunday must be celebrated in Latin. It would be a great help if the Consilium were to tell the whole Church how the Latin tongue can be preserved. If the Church is to remain truly the Catholic Church it is essential to keep a universal language.

5.   A very large number of Sisters and not a few parishes have dedicated their whole lives to perpetual adoration of the Blessed Sacrament. They sometimes feel anxious because of the danger that Exposition of the Blessed Sacrament and, perhaps, Benediction may one day be abolished on the grounds that they were introduced too recently in the history of the Church. A word of comfort and reassurance from the Consilium would be welcomed.

6.   I end by expressing, if I may, two thoughts about Synods of the future. I hope, in the first place, that Bishops' Conferences will be allowed to discuss the agenda with their clergy and faithful. I also hope that in the next Synod other bishops will take our place. In that way the views of the episcopate of the whole world are more likely to be heard.

Cardinal Heenan—Pastoral Letter, Advent 1967

John Carmel, Cardinal Priest of the Holy Roman Church of the title of San Silvestro in Capite, by the Grace of God and favour of the Apostolic See, Archbishop of Westminster and Metropolitan, to the Clergy and Faithful of the Diocese, health and blessing in the Lord.

Dearly Beloved Brethren in Christ:

At the Vatican Council there were nearly three thousand present and it was difficult to have real debates. At the recent Synod of Bishops our number was small enough for us to meet in a room in the Vatican. We were able to discuss questions intimately and thoroughly. The results of our meetings were passed to the Holy Father who will study them as soon as he has recovered from his operation. The Synod, as you know, was called to advise the Pope and no doubt he will announce his decisions in the coming year.

One of the subjects under discussion was the liturgy. Bishops from all over the world agreed that great benefits have come from the use of the mother tongue at Mass. People have begun to take a much more active part in the Holy Sacrifice. Children, especially, show great enthusiasm now that they follow the Mass in their own language. Many bishops, however, spoke of the loss to the whole Church if the Latin Mass were to disappear altogether. It would be tragic if the Catholic Church lacked a universal language for worship. It could come to be thought of as a national church in each country. I was glad to be able to tell the Synod that in Westminster we have a Latin Mass in every church each Sunday.

But whilst it is important not to let the Latin Mass die, it is no less important to make the English Mass as perfect as possible. At present it is rather a hotch-potch with its mixture of English and Latin. The Holy See has now given us leave to recite all the words of the Mass in English.

The Pope wants countries of the same language group to use the same translation. While the Council was still on we set up an international commission of priests and laymen who are experts either in the liturgy or the English language. It was their task to produce a translation acceptable to all the English speaking coun-tries. It is not easy for people familiar with the idiom of London, Washington or Sydney to agree on a com-mon text. That is one reason why we have had to wait so long for an agreed translation of the Canon, the most important part of the Mass. No trouble was spared in studying the best possible way of expressing the meaning of the Latin text in English.

The result is a translation which is accurate, clear and dignified. Listen carefully to the new translation. It takes time to become used to something new. So please don't make up your mind too quickly about the new version. We must give it a fair chance. If you don't like it the international committee for English in the Liturgy will be told to try again. This version, in any case, is experimental. The final reform of the liturgy is yet to come.

I hope, however, that this will be the last change for a long time. Bishop after bishop in the Synod rose to complain that his people are thoroughly tired of the constant changes. Don't imagine for a moment that your bishops approve change for the sake of change. We are most anxious to have done with the confusion which alterations in the Mass have brought about. Above all we want you to be left in peace to worship God in the way you know and love. But the reform was necessary. When we have the Mass in simple style with beautiful language all the annoyance caused by the experiments will prove to have been worth while [*sic*].

The Mass we are all looking forward to during these days is what used to be called Christ's Mass. That was the old name for Christmas. You will be in my three Masses and in all my prayers on Christmas Day. Please keep me in yours and ask God to give me the grace to serve Him and you well in the coming year. I thank you once again for the prayers you offered while I was ill. It is a real joy to be back again with my priests and people. May God bless every family in the diocese this Christmas and in the coming year.

Given at Westminster on the twenty-first day of November, the Feast of Our Lady's Presentation, in the year of Our

Lord nineteen hundred and sixty seven, and appointed to be read at every Mass, morning and evening, in all the churches and chapels of the Archdiocese on the First Sunday of Advent.[1]

+ John Cardinal Heenan
Archbishop of Westminster

[1] 3 December 1967.

Cardinal Heenan—Pastoral Letter on the New Liturgy and the Synod of Bishops

John Carmel, Cardinal Priest of the Holy Roman Church of the title of San Silvestro in Capite, by the Grace of God and favour of the Apostolic See, Archbishop of Westminster and Metropolitan, to the Clergy and Faithful of the Diocese, health and blessing in the Lord.

Dearly Beloved Brethren in Christ:

We have all heard people say: "Why can't they leave the Mass alone? Why all this chopping and changing?" This morning I want in a few words to tell you why.

The Council was clearly right to reform the liturgy. Take, for example, the use of English. Even those who know Latin have found that the words of the Mass mean more to them in their own language. It would, of course, be sad if the Council's determination to keep Latin as the language of the Roman rite were to be obstructed. That is why in Westminster diocese the parishes have at least one Latin Mass each Sunday— not that this alone will preserve the Latin liturgy. The present is no time for our Church to lose its universal language. Travel is no longer the monopoly of the rich. Many of you have been abroad—if only to Lourdes. I hope that Catholics everywhere will be able to sing the Credo together in Latin.

It is nevertheless a fact that use of the mother tongue has brought the Mass much closer to the people. Thus children can follow the Mass even before they learn to read a missal. The nuns who bake the altar breads tell me that parishes are continually increasing their orders. Thousands more are receiving Holy Communion regularly. That is one splendid result of the liturgical reforms.

That is true but it still does not answer the question "Why does the Mass keep changing?" Here is the answer. It would have been foolhardy to introduce the changes all at once. Some enthusiasts said that the bishops were "dragging their feet". But it was obviously wiser to change gradually and gently. If all the changes had been introduced together you would have been shocked. Now the final stage of the reform is about to be reached and you will experience no difficulty. Between now and Lent your priest will be giving several instructions on the liturgy. Its shape will remain much the same but the Mass will become simpler and a little shorter. There will be more variety in the Scripture readings and the congregation will be more united with the priest. Thus priest and people in future will recite the "I confess" together. That is an example of the sensible changes you will find in this final reform of the Mass.

When I speak of "final" reform I refer mainly to the Ordinary of the Mass in which there will probably be no further revision until, in the course of centuries, language and social customs require it. I do not suggest that the liturgy will now become completely rigid. There will, I hope, be new forms of the Mass devised for young children, the sick, the deaf and dumb, the blind and perhaps for other special groups. Beautiful new prayers for use at Baptism, Holy Matrimony and other sacraments are meanwhile being composed and translated. Liturgical progress will continue. Your Sunday Mass, however, will not be changed again in your lifetime. In a short time you will become familiar with the new Ordinary of the Mass and I am sure that you will appreciate it. Once more we shall have cause to thank God for the second Vatican Council. . . .[1]

Given at Westminster on the fifteenth day of September, the Feast of Our Lady of Sorrows, in the year of Our Lord nineteen hundred and sixty nine, and appointed to be read at every Mass, morning and evening, in all the churches and chapels of the Archdiocese on the Twentieth Sunday after Pentecost.[2]

+ John Cardinal Heenan
Archbishop of Westminster

---

[1] Cardinal Heenan then devotes two paragraphs to the forthcoming Synod of Bishops.

[2] 12 October 1969.

Cardinal Heenan—
Letter to Pope Paul VI*

Most Holy Father,

Thank you for receiving me so graciously this morning.

You asked me to send an informal note regarding the wish of many zealous Catholics—among whom are many converts—to be allowed on special occasions to use the old rite of Holy Mass. It is very difficult for them to give up the Latin Mass which they have learned to love in the old rite.

Most Catholics are quite happy with the new rite but some of the older people (like some of the older priests) would be grateful if they could occasionally have the so-called Tridentine Mass after it is officially withdrawn at the end of this year.

> Begging the Apostolic Blessing,
> Your affectionate son,
> John Card. Heenan.[1]

* 29 October 1971.

[1] The resultant "Heenan Indult", prepared by Father Bugnini, secretary of the Sacred Congregation for Divine Worship, on the explicit instructions of Paul VI, enabled English and Welsh bishops to permit the occasional use only of the *Ordo Missæ* as revised in 1965 and again in 1967. Bugnini states that the letter conveying this concession "urged that prudence and

reserve be exercised in granting the faculty and that any grant not be given too much publicity" (Annibale Bugnini, C.M., *The Reform of the Liturgy, 1948–1975* [Liturgical Press, 1990], p. 298). A decree of the English and Welsh bishops' conference dated 24 April 1975 and signed by Cardinal Heenan stated: "An indult was granted to the bishops of England and Wales to give permission to particular groups on special occasions to use the old rite as reformed in 1967. This permission was given on strict condition that all danger of division would be avoided. For devotional reasons a group may be given leave to have a Mass in this rite. At all parish and community Masses, however, the new rite is obligatory, whether it is in Latin or in English" (*Notitiæ* 11 [1975]: 143–44). In practice, such celebrations that occurred under the Heenan Indult used the unreformed preconciliar missal.

Afterword

Clare Asquith, Countess of Oxford

Evelyn Waugh has been accused of many failings, but timidity has never been one of them. It is difficult at this distance in time to recall the nerve it took to speak out as Waugh did, nearly fifty years ago in the *Spectator*, against the more exhilarating aspects of the "great wind" then sweeping through the Catholic Church as the Second Vatican Council began.[1] Hopes were high of the imminent reunion of Christendom, a project Waugh rejected as naïve and unrealistic. He had no time for the "Priesthood of the Laity", believing it would diminish the status of what he and Hilaire Belloc liked to call "the priest as a craftsman" with "an important job to do which none but he was qualified for".[2] The circular plans of modern churches such as the new Liverpool cathedral (likened by Waugh to a "surgical operating theatre") involved a congregation "staring at one another" and would bring reluctant worshippers no nearer the altar.[3] The movement to clarify the Mass would strip it of its mystery; as for the introduction of the vernacular, Waugh, the most

[1] Waugh, "The Same Again, Please", p. 34 above.
[2] Ibid., and Waugh's Easter 1964 diary entry, p. 52.
[3] Waugh, "The Same Again, Please", p. 36.

fastidious of stylists, had grim premonitions of the mixture of the banal and the archaic that would inevitably
replace the Latin. "Awe is the natural predisposition
to prayer", he wrote, fearing that if everything he heard
about the Council was true, the sense of awe would
be lost.[4] He knew he would be attacked as a reactionary, but as this book shows, he continued to oppose
the changes as they unfolded until his death. He lived
long enough to witness the experimental beginnings
of the new Mass, which Archbishop John Heenan
admitted was an "untidy mess",[5] and died a disillu-
sioned man for whom Mass-going had become a distasteful obligation, even a temptation to apostatise.

How many in England shared his views? His letter
to Katharine Asquith[6] implies that many did, including Heenan himself, but that as a group they were too
intimidated by the new movement to speak out. Powerful forces were ranged against them. Traditionalists
faced charges of ignorance from biblical scholars who
used new evidence to argue that the earliest and simplest Eucharistic rite was the most authentic; charges
of elitism from those for who saw Latin as an out-
dated barrier to the ignorant; and charges of self-centred
isolationism from ecumenists. Above all, traditional
Catholics were by their very nature the least likely to

[4] Ibid., p. 39.

[5] Archbishop Heenan to Waugh, 17 January 1965, p. 72.

[6] Letter dated 14 September 1964, p. 66. Katharine Asquith was the
daughter-in-law of H. H. Asquith, 1st Earl of Oxford and Asquith and
British prime minister from 1908 to 1916. Her husband, Raymond Asquith,
was killed in battle during World War I. Katharine became a Catholic in
1923.

raise their voices against the pope and the Council. Their complaints, however heartfelt, were made in private, and though some did indeed apostasise ("It is not I who have left the Church, it is the Church that has left me", pronounced one of Belloc's granddaughters), others, like Katharine Asquith's family, obediently complied, trusting that however radical and painful, reforms authorised by the papacy must in the end be guided by the Holy Spirit.

Nonetheless, for English Catholics in particular, the traditional form of the Latin Mass had a special significance. They could not let it go entirely. As Waugh pointed out, it was for the old rite rather than their Christian belief that the Elizabethan martyrs had died[7]— and it was for this form of the Mass that many English Catholic families had suffered centuries of persecution. Theirs was an awkward allegiance in the new atmosphere of ecumenical outreach. Accordingly, the petition forwarded by Heenan to Pope Paul VI in 1971 "to spare the traditional Latin Mass" explicitly avoided issues of doctrine, focussing instead on the Mass as an irreplaceable and beautiful human artefact comparable with the great cathedrals.[8] Perhaps if Waugh had lived long enough, he would have signed the petition. In a strategic move that would have amused him, the distinguished list of signatories included secular writers, Jewish artists, Anglican bishops, and only a discreet number of leading Catholics, including Katharine

---

[7] Waugh, "The Same Again, Please", p. 35.

[8] See the related letter of Cardinal Heenan to Pope Paul VI, 29 October 1971, pp. 112–13.

Asquith's son, Julian, 2nd Earl of Oxford and Asquith. The story goes that it was the inclusion of non-Catholic mystery writer Agatha Christie, whom Paul VI admired, that persuaded the pope to agree to what was then a unique national exemption—a detail Waugh might have invented himself.

Had the postconciliar Mass been generally accepted, Waugh's articles and what became known as the Agatha Christie indult would have been of historical interest only; however, even some of the reformers at the Second Vatican Council—including Joseph Ratzinger, now Pope Benedict XVI—have grave misgivings about some of the liturgical changes. The year before he became pope, Cardinal Ratzinger wrote that those who, like himself, were moved on the eve of the Council by the perception of the liturgy "as a living network of tradition" that awaited sensitive pruning by scholarly experts in order to flourish still further "can only stand, deeply sorrowing, before the ruins of the very things they were concerned for".[9]

There are other aspects of Waugh's shot across the bows in 1962 that now appear to be prescient rather than merely reactionary. Western Europe's vocations and congregations are in decline, and it is the traditionalists, not the liberals, of the Protestant churches who are turning to Catholicism. Under the papacy of Benedict XVI there are belated and contentious attempts to improve the inaccurate English translation of the

[9] Joseph Ratzinger, preface in Alcuin Reid, *The Organic Development of the Liturgy* (San Francisco: Ignatius Press, 2005), p. 11.

Novus Ordo; and there is a general awareness among English Catholics that the sacrificial aspect of the Mass and the mystery of the Real Presence, both deliberately marginalised in the interests of ecumenism, have indeed deteriorated, just as Waugh feared.

Waugh might have been still more vocal had he known how uncompromising some of the Council's most energetic reformers actually were. He was right to mistrust Heenan's reassurances that the changes "are not so great as they are made to appear".[10] In 1965, the year before Waugh's death, Father (later Archbishop) Annibale Bugnini, secretary of the commission that oversaw the changes made to the Mass, was urging, "We must strip from our Catholic prayers and our Catholic liturgy everything which can be the shadow of a stumbling block for our separated brethren, that is, for Protestants."[11] Nine years later, he announced with satisfaction that the ensuing reform was "a major conquest of the Roman Catholic Church".[12] The French Jesuit and composer Joseph Gelineau confirmed: "To tell the truth it is a different liturgy of the Mass. . . . The Roman Rite as we knew it no longer exists. It has been destroyed."[13]

One of the congratulatory letters on Waugh's first article in the *Spectator* is from the bishop of Leeds, who

---

[10] Archbishop Heenan to Waugh, 20 August 1964, p. 62.

[11] *L'Osservatore Romano*, 19 March 1965, quoted in Michael Davies, "Annibale Bugnini: The Main Author of the Novus Ordo", http://www.catholicapologetics.info/modernproblems/newmass/bugnini.html.

[12] Quoted in Davies, "Annibale Bugnini".

[13] Joseph Gelineau, *Demain la liturgie* (Cerf, 1976), quoted in Davies, "Annibale Bugnini".

regrets that Waugh's protests, though well founded, came too late. A year earlier he might have galvanised "the inarticulate faithful" against the "articulate few".[14] Heenan said much the same, agreeing with everything in the article and lamenting, "What a pity the voice of the laity was not heard sooner."[15] But were they right? Is it really true that the clergy were misled by an articulate minority into believing that most of the faithful were unhappy with the old Mass and were yearning for wholesale liturgical reform? The Catholic Church is not a democracy, and it is impossible to judge just how many silent worshippers sided with Waugh and how many with the liberals. But it is interesting to note that both Heenan and Ratzinger afterwards identified one of the main weaknesses of the Council as a failure to listen to ordinary parish priests and laity in preference to specialists and experts. Where Bugnini and other reformers concentrated on ecumenical unity at all costs, Ratzinger chose language closer to Waugh's: "Liturgy is not about us, but about God. Forgetting about God is the most imminent danger of our age.... What happens if the habit of forgetting about God makes itself at home in the Liturgy itself ... ?"[16]

---

[14] Archbishop Heenan to Evelyn Waugh, 25 November 1962, p. 43, footnote 1.

[15] Ibid., p. 42.

[16] Ratzinger, preface in Reid, *Organic Development of the Liturgy*, p. 13.

Appendix

The 1971 Petition to Pope Paul VI By Distinguished Writers, Scholars, Artists, and Historians Living in England to Spare the Traditional Latin Mass

If some senseless decree were to order the total or partial destruction of basilicas or cathedrals, then obviously it would be the educated—whatever their personal beliefs—who would rise up in horror to oppose such a possibility.

Now the fact is that basilicas and cathedrals were built so as to celebrate a rite which, until a few months ago, constituted a living tradition. We are referring to the Roman Catholic Mass. Yet, according to the latest information in Rome, there is a plan to obliterate that Mass by the end of the current year.

One of the axioms of contemporary publicity, religious as well as secular, is that modern man in general, and intellectuals in particular, have become intolerant of all forms of tradition and are anxious to suppress them and put something else in their place.

But, like many other affirmations of our publicity machines, this axiom is false. Today, as in times gone by, educated people are in the vanguard where recognition of the value of tradition is concerned, and are the first to raise the alarm when it is threatened.

We are not at this moment considering the religious or spiritual experience of millions of individuals. The rite in question, in its magnificent Latin text, has also inspired a host of priceless achievements in the arts—not only mystical works, but works by poets, philosophers, musicians, architects, painters and sculptors in all countries and epochs. Thus, it belongs to universal culture as well as to churchmen and formal Christians.

In the materialistic and technocratic civilisation that is increasingly threatening the life of mind and spirit in its original creative expression—the word—it seems particularly inhuman to deprive man of word-forms in one of their most grandiose manifestations.

The signatories of this appeal, which is entirely ecumenical and nonpolitical, have been drawn from every branch of modern culture in Europe and elsewhere. They wish to call to the attention of the Holy See the appalling responsibility it would incur in the history of the human spirit were it to refuse to allow the Traditional Mass to survive, even though this survival took place side by side with other liturgical forms.

Signed,

Harold Acton
Vladimir Ashkenazy
John Bayler
Lennox Berkeley
Maurice Bowra

Agatha Christie
Kenneth Clark
Nevill Coghill
Cyril Connolly
Colin Davis
Hugh Delargy
Robert Exeter
Miles Fitzalen-Howard
Constantine Fitzgibbon
William Glock
Magdalen Goftlin
Robert Graves
Graham Greene
Ian Greenless
Joseph Grimond
Harman Grisewood
Colin Hardie
Rupert Hart-Davis
Barbara Hepworth
Auberon Herbert
John Jolliffe
David Jones
Osbert Lancaster
F. R. Leavis
Cecil Day Lewis
Compton Mackenzie
George Malcolm
Max Mallowan
Alfred Marnau
Yehudi Menuhin
Nancy Mitford

Raymond Mortimer
Malcolm Muggeridge
Iris Murdoch
John Murray
Sean O'Faolain
E. J. Oliver
Oxford and Asquith
William Plomer
Kathleen Raine
William Rees-Mogg
Ralph Richardson
John Ripon
Charles Russell
Rivers Scott
Joan Sutherland
Philip Toynbee
Martin Turnell
Bernard Wall
Patrick Wall
E. I. Watkin
R. C. Zaehner